FOOTBALL

Scouting Notebook

TEMPLATES FOR SCOUTING REPORTS OF FOOTBALL PLAYERS

FOOTBALL

TEMPLATES FOR SCOUTING REPORTS OF FOOTBALL PLAYERS
Wanceulen Editorial
Editorial collection: Wanceulen Notebook
© Wanceulen Editorial S. L.
Web: www.wanceulen.com y www.wanceuleneditorial.com
Email: info@wanceuleneditorial.com
c/ Cristo del Desamparo y Abandono, 56 – 41006 Sevilla (Spain)

All rights reserved. It is forbidden to reproduce this work. No parts may be reproduced, stored or be transmitted in any form or by any means, electronic, mechanic, photocopying, recording of otherwise without written permission of the owners of the intellectual property rights

Write the players' data of the matches you see.

REGISTRATION TEMPLATES FOR 30 FOOTBALL MATCHES

How to use it:

Each MATCH consists of 4 registration pages:

- **The first two pages** are for the registration of the players of each team: **names, numbers, demarcation and basic general characteristics of each player**. At the bottom of the page there are playfields to help us graphically place players.

- The next two pages (3 and 4) include a table with boxes so you can take **the notes you consider about the players that have excelled in each team** and about which you think it is worth expanding the information basic that you have written down in the previous record sheet.

- From each game you can also record the reference data: **teams participating, category and competition, day and time, and field** where the game is played.

- **It supposes a useful registry of data that you can file**, before computerizing them, or before passing them to the archives or databases where you store the information of your observations.

TEAM	-	
CATEGORY	COMPETITION	

TEAM _____

N	PLAYER	DEM.	FIRST GLANCE
1.			
2.			
3.			
4.			
5.			
6.			
7.			
8.			
9.			
10.			
11.			
12.			
13.			
14.			
15.			
16.			
17.			
18.			

DATE	TIME	FIELD
Observation (direct / video):		

Referencias de jugadores/as del EQUIPO _____

N	PLAYER	DEM.	FIRST GLANCE
1.			
2.			
3.			
4.			
5.			
6.			
7.			
8.			
9.			
10.			
11.			
12.			
13.			
14.			
15.			
16.			
17.			
18.			

MATCH	-
CATEGORY	COMPETITION

TEAM _____

PLAYER:	PLAYER:

PLAYER:	PLAYER:

PLAYER:	PLAYER:

DATE	TIME	FIELD

TEAM _____

PLAYER:	PLAYER:

PLAYER:	PLAYER:

PLAYER:	PLAYER:

TEAM	-		
CATEGORY		COMPETITION	

TEAM _____

N	PLAYER	DEM.	FIRST GLANCE
1.			
2.			
3.			
4.			
5.			
6.			
7.			
8.			
9.			
10.			
11.			
12.			
13.			
14.			
15.			
16.			
17.			
18.			

DATE	TIME	FIELD
Observation (direct / video):		

Referencias de jugadores/as del EQUIPO _____

N	PLAYER	DEM.	FIRST GLANCE
1.			
2.			
3.			
4.			
5.			
6.			
7.			
8.			
9.			
10.			
11.			
12.			
13.			
14.			
15.			
16.			
17.			
18.			

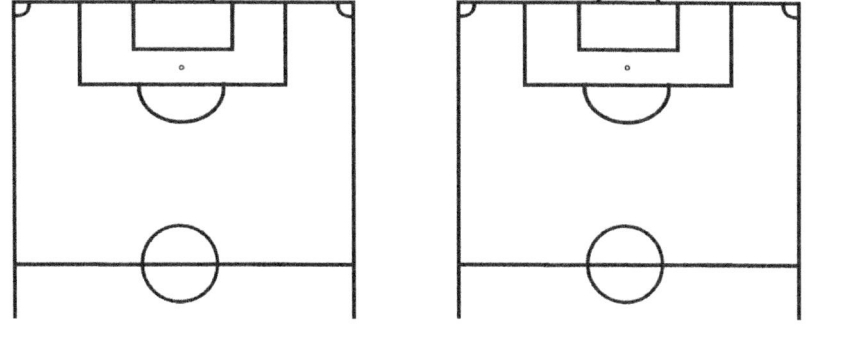

MATCH	-
CATEGORY	COMPETITION

TEAM _____

PLAYER:	PLAYER:

PLAYER:	PLAYER:

PLAYER:	PLAYER:

DATE	TIME	FIELD

TEAM _____

PLAYER:

PLAYER:

PLAYER:

PLAYER:

PLAYER:

PLAYER:

TEAM	-	
CATEGORY	COMPETITION	

TEAM _____

N	PLAYER	DEM.	FIRST GLANCE
1.			
2.			
3.			
4.			
5.			
6.			
7.			
8.			
9.			
10.			
11.			
12.			
13.			
14.			
15.			
16.			
17.			
18.			

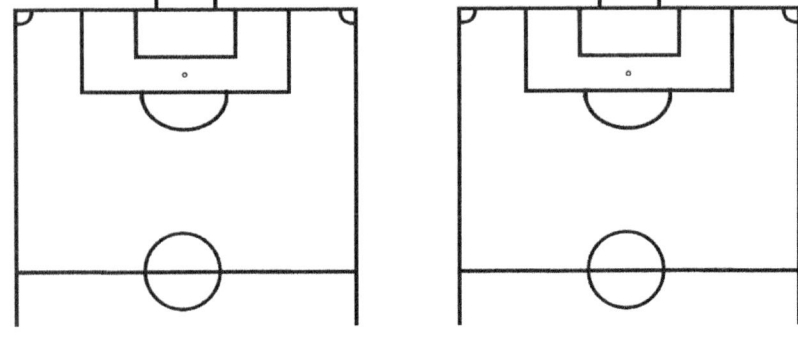

DATE		TIME		FIELD	
Observation (direct / video):					

Referencias de jugadores/as del EQUIPO _____

N	PLAYER	DEM.	FIRST GLANCE
1.			
2.			
3.			
4.			
5.			
6.			
7.			
8.			
9.			
10.			
11.			
12.			
13.			
14.			
15.			
16.			
17.			
18.			

MATCH	-
CATEGORY	COMPETITION

TEAM _____

PLAYER:	PLAYER:

PLAYER:	PLAYER:

PLAYER:	PLAYER:

DATE	TIME	FIELD

TEAM _____

PLAYER:

PLAYER:

PLAYER:

PLAYER:

PLAYER:

PLAYER:

TEAM		-	
CATEGORY		COMPETITION	

TEAM _____

N	PLAYER	DEM.	FIRST GLANCE
1.			
2.			
3.			
4.			
5.			
6.			
7.			
8.			
9.			
10.			
11.			
12.			
13.			
14.			
15.			
16.			
17.			
18.			

DATE	TIME	FIELD
Observation (direct / video):		

Referencias de jugadores/as del EQUIPO _____

N	PLAYER	DEM.	FIRST GLANCE
1.			
2.			
3.			
4.			
5.			
6.			
7.			
8.			
9.			
10.			
11.			
12.			
13.			
14.			
15.			
16.			
17.			
18.			

MATCH	-
CATEGORY	COMPETITION

TEAM _____

PLAYER:	PLAYER:

PLAYER:	PLAYER:

PLAYER:	PLAYER:

| DATE | TIME | FIELD |

TEAM _____

PLAYER:	PLAYER:

PLAYER:	PLAYER:

PLAYER:	PLAYER:

TEAM	-
CATEGORY	COMPETITION

TEAM _____

N	PLAYER	DEM.	FIRST GLANCE
1.			
2.			
3.			
4.			
5.			
6.			
7.			
8.			
9.			
10.			
11.			
12.			
13.			
14.			
15.			
16.			
17.			
18.			

DATE	TIME	FIELD
Observation (direct / video):		

Referencias de jugadores/as del EQUIPO _____

N	PLAYER	DEM.	FIRST GLANCE
1.			
2.			
3.			
4.			
5.			
6.			
7.			
8.			
9.			
10.			
11.			
12.			
13.			
14.			
15.			
16.			
17.			
18.			

MATCH	-
CATEGORY	COMPETITION

TEAM _____

PLAYER:	PLAYER:

PLAYER:	PLAYER:

PLAYER:	PLAYER:

DATE	TIME	FIELD

TEAM _____

PLAYER:	PLAYER:

PLAYER:	PLAYER:

PLAYER:	PLAYER:

TEAM	-	
CATEGORY	COMPETITION	

TEAM _____

N	PLAYER	DEM.	FIRST GLANCE
1.			
2.			
3.			
4.			
5.			
6.			
7.			
8.			
9.			
10.			
11.			
12.			
13.			
14.			
15.			
16.			
17.			
18.			

DATE	TIME	FIELD
Observation (direct / video):		

Referencias de jugadores/as del EQUIPO _____

N	PLAYER	DEM.	FIRST GLANCE
1.			
2.			
3.			
4.			
5.			
6.			
7.			
8.			
9.			
10.			
11.			
12.			
13.			
14.			
15.			
16.			
17.			
18.			

MATCH	-
CATEGORY	COMPETITION

TEAM _____

PLAYER:	PLAYER:

PLAYER:	PLAYER:

PLAYER:	PLAYER:

DATE	TIME	FIELD

TEAM _____

PLAYER:	PLAYER:

PLAYER:	PLAYER:

PLAYER:	PLAYER:

TEAM	-	
CATEGORY	COMPETITION	

TEAM _____

N	PLAYER	DEM.	FIRST GLANCE
1.			
2.			
3.			
4.			
5.			
6.			
7.			
8.			
9.			
10.			
11.			
12.			
13.			
14.			
15.			
16.			
17.			
18.			

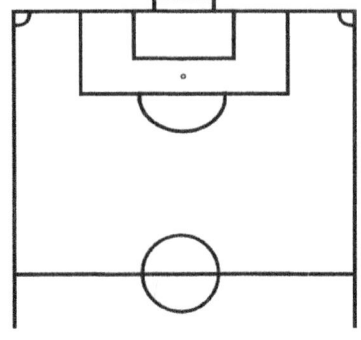
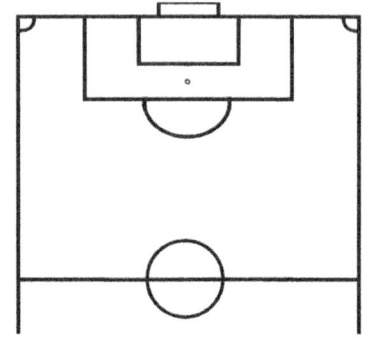

DATE	TIME	FIELD
Observation (direct / video):		

Referencias de jugadores/as del EQUIPO _____

N	PLAYER	DEM.	FIRST GLANCE
1.			
2.			
3.			
4.			
5.			
6.			
7.			
8.			
9.			
10.			
11.			
12.			
13.			
14.			
15.			
16.			
17.			
18.			

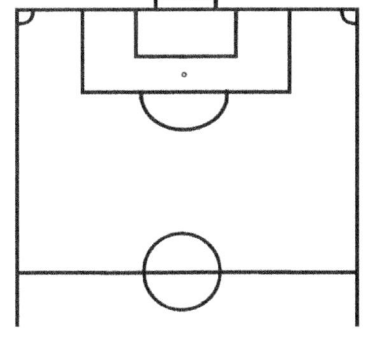
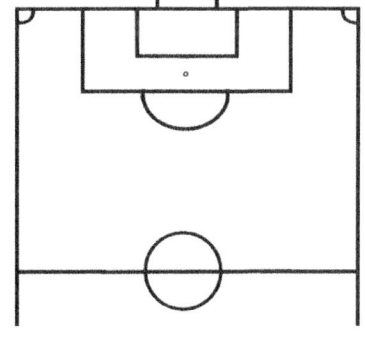

MATCH	-
CATEGORY	COMPETITION

TEAM _____

PLAYER:	PLAYER:

PLAYER:	PLAYER:

PLAYER:	PLAYER:

DATE	TIME	FIELD

TEAM _____

PLAYER:	PLAYER:

PLAYER:	PLAYER:

PLAYER:	PLAYER:

TEAM	-
CATEGORY	COMPETITION

TEAM _____

N	PLAYER	DEM.	FIRST GLANCE
1.			
2.			
3.			
4.			
5.			
6.			
7.			
8.			
9.			
10.			
11.			
12.			
13.			
14.			
15.			
16.			
17.			
18.			

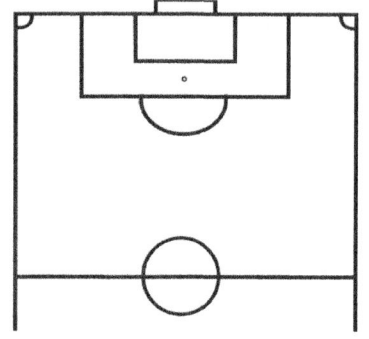

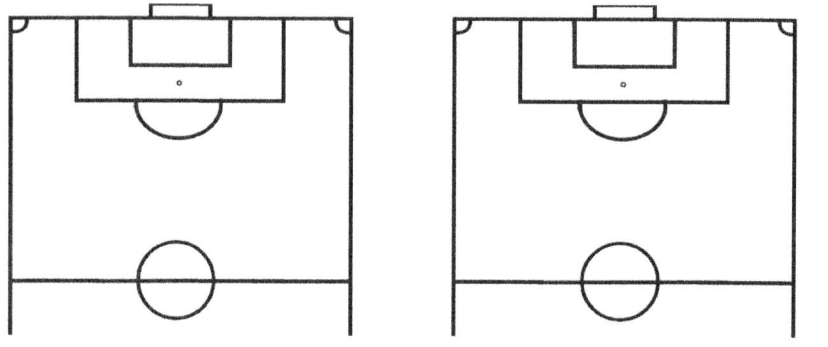

DATE	TIME	FIELD
Observation (direct / video):		

Referencias de jugadores/as del EQUIPO _____

N	PLAYER	DEM.	FIRST GLANCE
1.			
2.			
3.			
4.			
5.			
6.			
7.			
8.			
9.			
10.			
11.			
12.			
13.			
14.			
15.			
16.			
17.			
18.			

MATCH	-
CATEGORY	COMPETITION

TEAM _____

PLAYER:

PLAYER:

PLAYER:

PLAYER:

PLAYER:

PLAYER:

DATE	TIME	FIELD

TEAM _____

PLAYER:	PLAYER:

PLAYER:	PLAYER:

PLAYER:	PLAYER:

TEAM	-	
CATEGORY	COMPETITION	

TEAM _____

N	PLAYER	DEM.	FIRST GLANCE
1.			
2.			
3.			
4.			
5.			
6.			
7.			
8.			
9.			
10.			
11.			
12.			
13.			
14.			
15.			
16.			
17.			
18.			

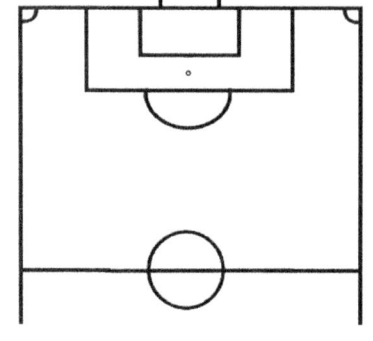
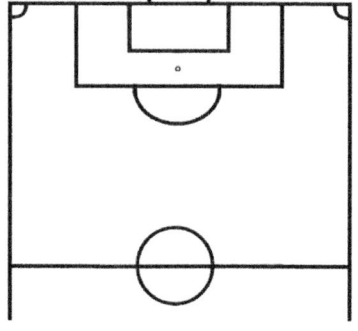

DATE		TIME		FIELD	
Observation (direct / video):					

Referencias de jugadores/as del EQUIPO _____

N	PLAYER	DEM.	FIRST GLANCE
1.			
2.			
3.			
4.			
5.			
6.			
7.			
8.			
9.			
10.			
11.			
12.			
13.			
14.			
15.			
16.			
17.			
18.			

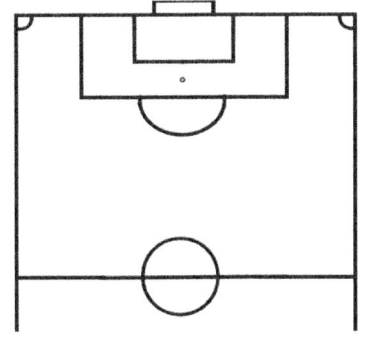

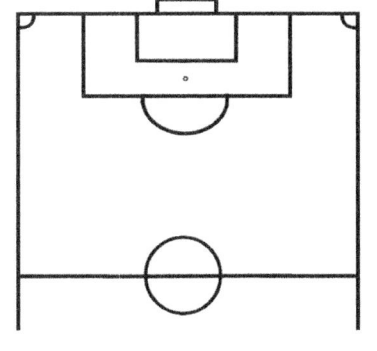

MATCH	-
CATEGORY	COMPETITION

TEAM _____

PLAYER:	PLAYER:

PLAYER:	PLAYER:

PLAYER:	PLAYER:

DATE	TIME	FIELD

TEAM _____

PLAYER:	PLAYER:

PLAYER:	PLAYER:

PLAYER:	PLAYER:

TEAM	-	
CATEGORY	COMPETITION	

TEAM _____

N	PLAYER	DEM.	FIRST GLANCE
1.			
2.			
3.			
4.			
5.			
6.			
7.			
8.			
9.			
10.			
11.			
12.			
13.			
14.			
15.			
16.			
17.			
18.			

DATE		TIME		FIELD	
Observation (direct / video):					

Referencias de jugadores/as del EQUIPO _____

N	PLAYER	DEM.	FIRST GLANCE
1.			
2.			
3.			
4.			
5.			
6.			
7.			
8.			
9.			
10.			
11.			
12.			
13.			
14.			
15.			
16.			
17.			
18.			

MATCH	-
CATEGORY	COMPETITION

TEAM _____

PLAYER:	PLAYER:

PLAYER:	PLAYER:

PLAYER:	PLAYER:

DATE	TIME	FIELD

TEAM _____

PLAYER:	**PLAYER:**

PLAYER:	**PLAYER:**

PLAYER:	**PLAYER:**

TEAM	-
CATEGORY	COMPETITION

TEAM _____

N	PLAYER	DEM.	FIRST GLANCE
1.			
2.			
3.			
4.			
5.			
6.			
7.			
8.			
9.			
10.			
11.			
12.			
13.			
14.			
15.			
16.			
17.			
18.			

DATE	TIME	FIELD
Observation (direct / video):		

Referencias de jugadores/as del EQUIPO _____

N	PLAYER	DEM.	FIRST GLANCE
1.			
2.			
3.			
4.			
5.			
6.			
7.			
8.			
9.			
10.			
11.			
12.			
13.			
14.			
15.			
16.			
17.			
18.			

MATCH	-
CATEGORY	COMPETITION

TEAM _____

PLAYER:	PLAYER:

PLAYER:	PLAYER:

PLAYER:	PLAYER:

DATE	TIME	FIELD

TEAM _____

PLAYER:	PLAYER:

PLAYER:	PLAYER:

PLAYER:	PLAYER:

TEAM	-	
CATEGORY	COMPETITION	

TEAM _____

N	PLAYER	DEM.	FIRST GLANCE
1.			
2.			
3.			
4.			
5.			
6.			
7.			
8.			
9.			
10.			
11.			
12.			
13.			
14.			
15.			
16.			
17.			
18.			

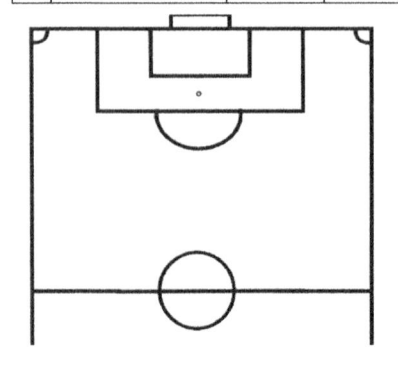

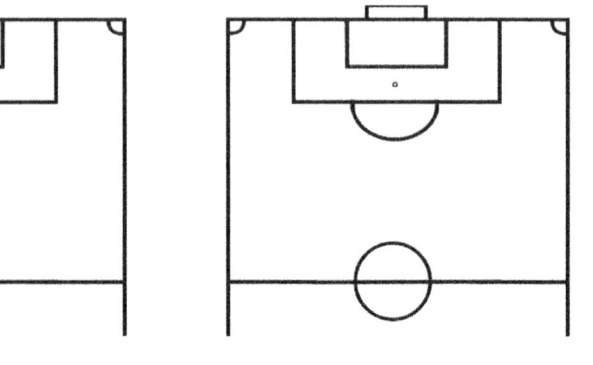

DATE	TIME	FIELD
Observation (direct / video):		

Referencias de jugadores/as del EQUIPO _____

N	PLAYER	DEM.	FIRST GLANCE
1.			
2.			
3.			
4.			
5.			
6.			
7.			
8.			
9.			
10.			
11.			
12.			
13.			
14.			
15.			
16.			
17.			
18.			

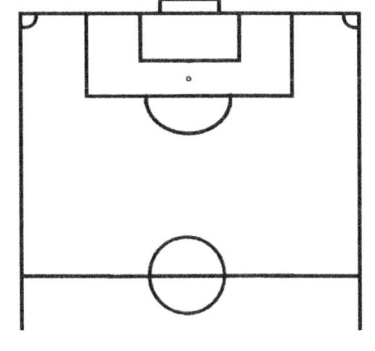

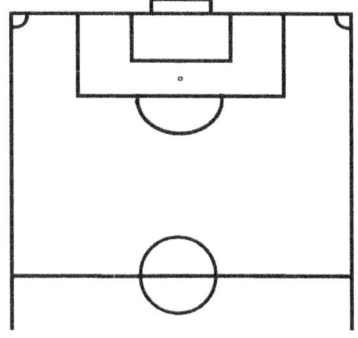

MATCH	-
CATEGORY	COMPETITION

TEAM _____

PLAYER:	PLAYER:

PLAYER:	PLAYER:

PLAYER:	PLAYER:

DATE	TIME	FIELD

TEAM _____

PLAYER:	PLAYER:

PLAYER:	PLAYER:

PLAYER:	PLAYER:

TEAM	-
CATEGORY	COMPETITION

TEAM _____

N	PLAYER	DEM.	FIRST GLANCE
1.			
2.			
3.			
4.			
5.			
6.			
7.			
8.			
9.			
10.			
11.			
12.			
13.			
14.			
15.			
16.			
17.			
18.			

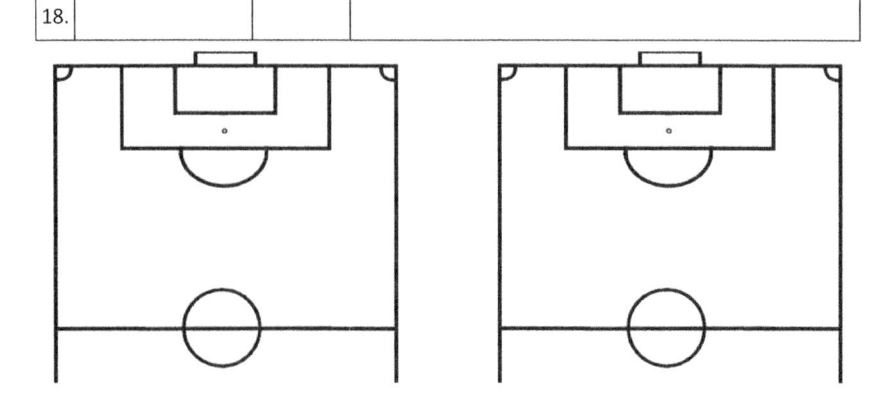

DATE	TIME	FIELD
Observation (direct / video):		

Referencias de jugadores/as del EQUIPO _____

N	PLAYER	DEM.	FIRST GLANCE
1.			
2.			
3.			
4.			
5.			
6.			
7.			
8.			
9.			
10.			
11.			
12.			
13.			
14.			
15.			
16.			
17.			
18.			

MATCH	-
CATEGORY	COMPETITION

TEAM _____

PLAYER:	PLAYER:

PLAYER:	PLAYER:

PLAYER:	PLAYER:

DATE	TIME	FIELD

TEAM _____

PLAYER:	PLAYER:

PLAYER:	PLAYER:

PLAYER:	PLAYER:

TEAM	-	
CATEGORY	COMPETITION	

TEAM _____

N	PLAYER	DEM.	FIRST GLANCE
1.			
2.			
3.			
4.			
5.			
6.			
7.			
8.			
9.			
10.			
11.			
12.			
13.			
14.			
15.			
16.			
17.			
18.			

DATE	TIME	FIELD
Observation (direct / video):		

Referencias de jugadores/as del EQUIPO _____

N	PLAYER	DEM.	FIRST GLANCE
1.			
2.			
3.			
4.			
5.			
6.			
7.			
8.			
9.			
10.			
11.			
12.			
13.			
14.			
15.			
16.			
17.			
18.			

MATCH	-
CATEGORY	COMPETITION

TEAM _____

PLAYER:	PLAYER:

PLAYER:	PLAYER:

PLAYER:	PLAYER:

DATE	TIME	FIELD

TEAM _____

PLAYER:	PLAYER:

PLAYER:	PLAYER:

PLAYER:	PLAYER:

TEAM	-		
CATEGORY		COMPETITION	

TEAM _____

N	PLAYER	DEM.	FIRST GLANCE
1.			
2.			
3.			
4.			
5.			
6.			
7.			
8.			
9.			
10.			
11.			
12.			
13.			
14.			
15.			
16.			
17.			
18.			

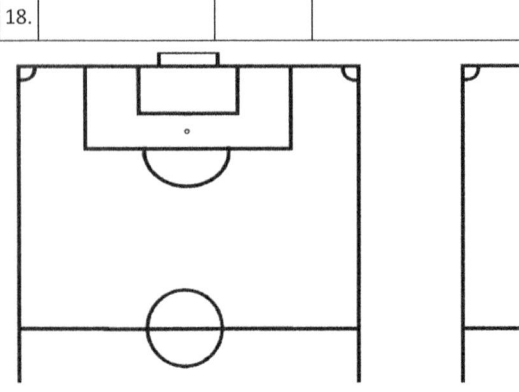

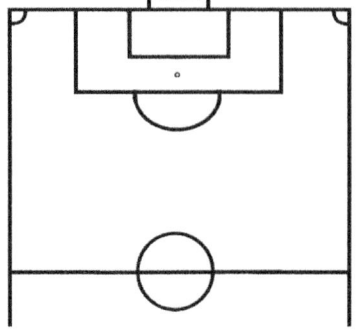

DATE	TIME	FIELD
Observation (direct / video):		

Referencias de jugadores/as del EQUIPO _____

N	PLAYER	DEM.	FIRST GLANCE
1.			
2.			
3.			
4.			
5.			
6.			
7.			
8.			
9.			
10.			
11.			
12.			
13.			
14.			
15.			
16.			
17.			
18.			

MATCH	-
CATEGORY	COMPETITION

TEAM _____

PLAYER:	PLAYER:

PLAYER:	PLAYER:

PLAYER:	PLAYER:

DATE	TIME	FIELD

TEAM _____

PLAYER:	PLAYER:
PLAYER:	PLAYER:
PLAYER:	PLAYER:

TEAM	-	
CATEGORY	COMPETITION	

TEAM _____

N	PLAYER	DEM.	FIRST GLANCE
1.			
2.			
3.			
4.			
5.			
6.			
7.			
8.			
9.			
10.			
11.			
12.			
13.			
14.			
15.			
16.			
17.			
18.			

DATE	TIME	FIELD
Observation (direct / video):		

Referencias de jugadores/as del EQUIPO _____

N	PLAYER	DEM.	FIRST GLANCE
1.			
2.			
3.			
4.			
5.			
6.			
7.			
8.			
9.			
10.			
11.			
12.			
13.			
14.			
15.			
16.			
17.			
18.			

MATCH	-
CATEGORY	COMPETITION

TEAM _____

PLAYER:	PLAYER:

PLAYER:	PLAYER:

PLAYER:	PLAYER:

DATE	TIME	FIELD

TEAM _____

PLAYER:	PLAYER:
PLAYER:	**PLAYER:**
PLAYER:	**PLAYER:**

TEAM	-
CATEGORY	COMPETITION

TEAM _____

N	PLAYER	DEM.	FIRST GLANCE
1.			
2.			
3.			
4.			
5.			
6.			
7.			
8.			
9.			
10.			
11.			
12.			
13.			
14.			
15.			
16.			
17.			
18.			

DATE	TIME	FIELD
Observation (direct / video):		

Referencias de jugadores/as del EQUIPO _____

N	PLAYER	DEM.	FIRST GLANCE
1.			
2.			
3.			
4.			
5.			
6.			
7.			
8.			
9.			
10.			
11.			
12.			
13.			
14.			
15.			
16.			
17.			
18.			

MATCH	-
CATEGORY	COMPETITION

TEAM _____

PLAYER:	PLAYER:

PLAYER:	PLAYER:

PLAYER:	PLAYER:

DATE	TIME	FIELD

TEAM _____

PLAYER:	PLAYER:

PLAYER:	PLAYER:

PLAYER:	PLAYER:

TEAM	-		
CATEGORY		COMPETITION	

TEAM _____

N	PLAYER	DEM.	FIRST GLANCE
1.			
2.			
3.			
4.			
5.			
6.			
7.			
8.			
9.			
10.			
11.			
12.			
13.			
14.			
15.			
16.			
17.			
18.			

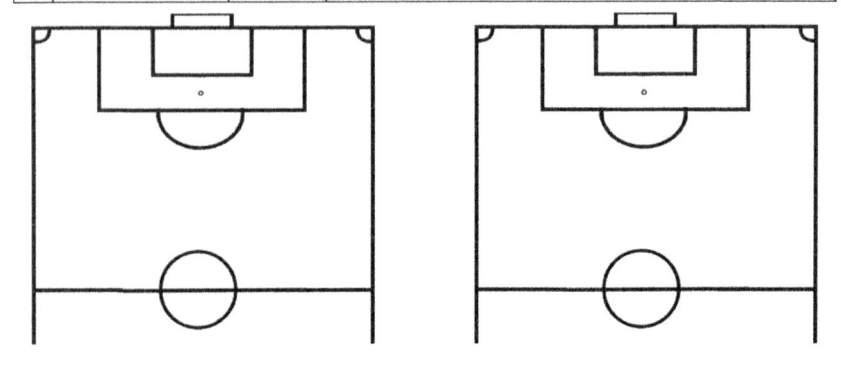

DATE	TIME	FIELD
Observation (direct / video):		

Referencias de jugadores/as del EQUIPO _____

N	PLAYER	DEM.	FIRST GLANCE
1.			
2.			
3.			
4.			
5.			
6.			
7.			
8.			
9.			
10.			
11.			
12.			
13.			
14.			
15.			
16.			
17.			
18.			

MATCH	-
CATEGORY	COMPETITION

TEAM _____

PLAYER:	PLAYER:

PLAYER:	PLAYER:

PLAYER:	PLAYER:

DATE	TIME	FIELD

TEAM _____

PLAYER:	PLAYER:
PLAYER:	PLAYER:
PLAYER:	PLAYER:

TEAM	-
CATEGORY	COMPETITION

TEAM _____

N	PLAYER	DEM.	FIRST GLANCE
1.			
2.			
3.			
4.			
5.			
6.			
7.			
8.			
9.			
10.			
11.			
12.			
13.			
14.			
15.			
16.			
17.			
18.			

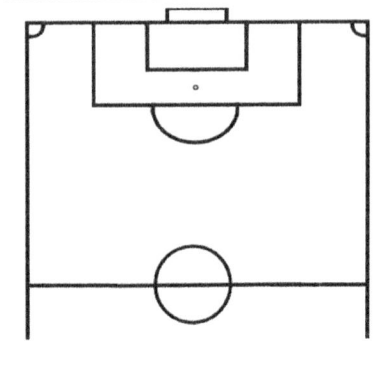

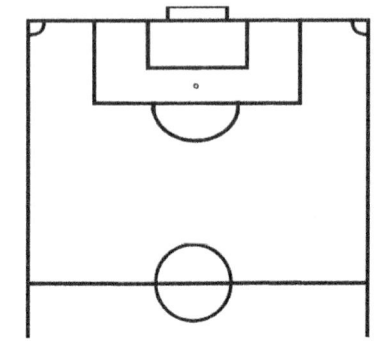

DATE	TIME	FIELD
Observation (direct / video):		

Referencias de jugadores/as del EQUIPO _____

N	PLAYER	DEM.	FIRST GLANCE
1.			
2.			
3.			
4.			
5.			
6.			
7.			
8.			
9.			
10.			
11.			
12.			
13.			
14.			
15.			
16.			
17.			
18.			

MATCH	-
CATEGORY	COMPETITION

TEAM _____

PLAYER:	PLAYER:

PLAYER:	PLAYER:

PLAYER:	PLAYER:

DATE	TIME	FIELD

TEAM _____

PLAYER:	PLAYER:

PLAYER:	PLAYER:

PLAYER:	PLAYER:

TEAM	-
CATEGORY	COMPETITION

TEAM _____

N	PLAYER	DEM.	FIRST GLANCE
1.			
2.			
3.			
4.			
5.			
6.			
7.			
8.			
9.			
10.			
11.			
12.			
13.			
14.			
15.			
16.			
17.			
18.			

DATE	TIME	FIELD
Observation (direct / video):		

Referencias de jugadores/as del EQUIPO _____

N	PLAYER	DEM.	FIRST GLANCE
1.			
2.			
3.			
4.			
5.			
6.			
7.			
8.			
9.			
10.			
11.			
12.			
13.			
14.			
15.			
16.			
17.			
18.			

MATCH	-
CATEGORY	COMPETITION

TEAM _____

PLAYER:	PLAYER:

PLAYER:	PLAYER:

PLAYER:	PLAYER:

DATE	TIME	FIELD

TEAM _____

PLAYER:	PLAYER:

PLAYER:	PLAYER:

PLAYER:	PLAYER:

TEAM	-
CATEGORY	COMPETITION

TEAM _____

N	PLAYER	DEM.	FIRST GLANCE
1.			
2.			
3.			
4.			
5.			
6.			
7.			
8.			
9.			
10.			
11.			
12.			
13.			
14.			
15.			
16.			
17.			
18.			

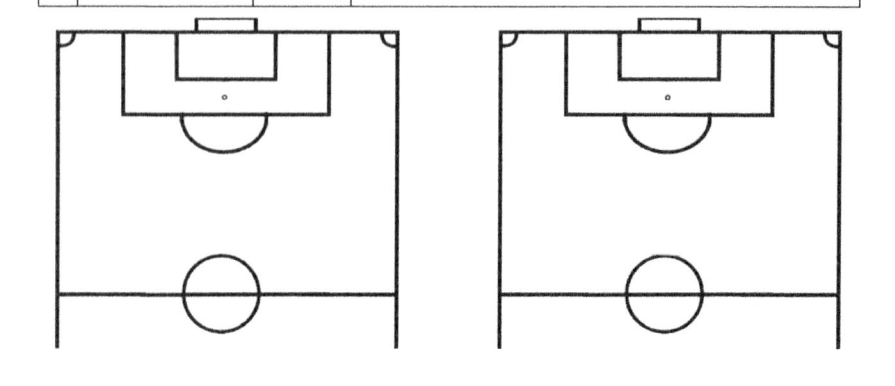

DATE	TIME	FIELD
Observation (direct / video):		

Referencias de jugadores/as del EQUIPO _____

N	PLAYER	DEM.	FIRST GLANCE
1.			
2.			
3.			
4.			
5.			
6.			
7.			
8.			
9.			
10.			
11.			
12.			
13.			
14.			
15.			
16.			
17.			
18.			

MATCH	-
CATEGORY	COMPETITION

TEAM _____

PLAYER:	PLAYER:

PLAYER:	PLAYER:

PLAYER:	PLAYER:

DATE	TIME	FIELD

TEAM _____

PLAYER:	PLAYER:

PLAYER:	PLAYER:

PLAYER:	PLAYER:

TEAM	-
CATEGORY	COMPETITION

TEAM _____

N	PLAYER	DEM.	FIRST GLANCE
1.			
2.			
3.			
4.			
5.			
6.			
7.			
8.			
9.			
10.			
11.			
12.			
13.			
14.			
15.			
16.			
17.			
18.			

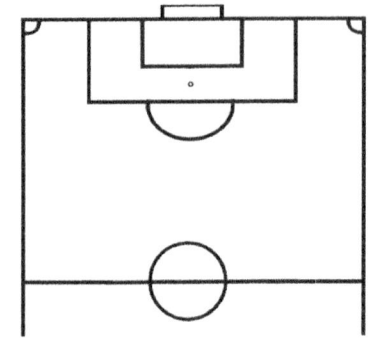

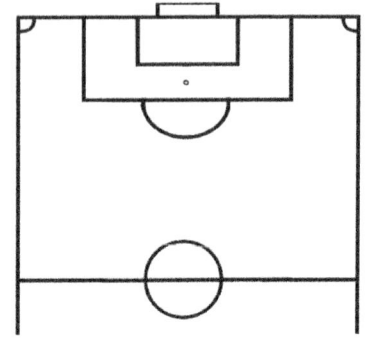

DATE	TIME	FIELD
Observation (direct / video):		

Referencias de jugadores/as del EQUIPO _____

N	PLAYER	DEM.	FIRST GLANCE
1.			
2.			
3.			
4.			
5.			
6.			
7.			
8.			
9.			
10.			
11.			
12.			
13.			
14.			
15.			
16.			
17.			
18.			

MATCH	-
CATEGORY	COMPETITION

TEAM _____

PLAYER:	PLAYER:

PLAYER:	PLAYER:

PLAYER:	PLAYER:

DATE	TIME	FIELD

TEAM _____

PLAYER:	PLAYER:

PLAYER:	PLAYER:

PLAYER:	PLAYER:

TEAM	-	
CATEGORY	COMPETITION	

TEAM _____

N	PLAYER	DEM.	FIRST GLANCE
1.			
2.			
3.			
4.			
5.			
6.			
7.			
8.			
9.			
10.			
11.			
12.			
13.			
14.			
15.			
16.			
17.			
18.			

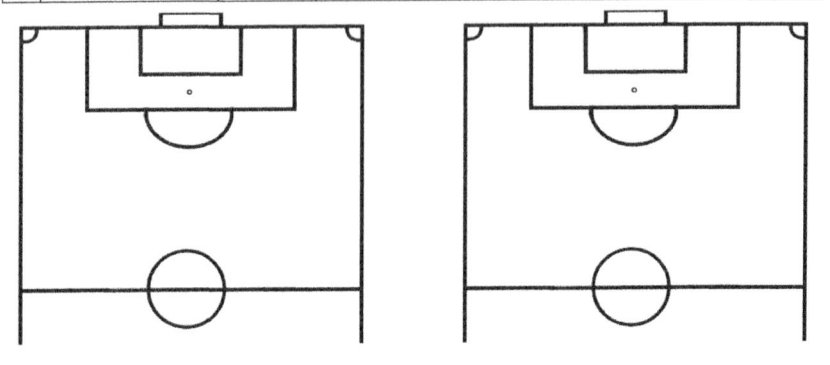

DATE		TIME		FIELD	
Observation (direct / video):					

Referencias de jugadores/as del EQUIPO _____

N	PLAYER	DEM.	FIRST GLANCE
1.			
2.			
3.			
4.			
5.			
6.			
7.			
8.			
9.			
10.			
11.			
12.			
13.			
14.			
15.			
16.			
17.			
18.			

MATCH	-
CATEGORY	COMPETITION

TEAM _____

PLAYER:	PLAYER:

PLAYER:	PLAYER:

PLAYER:	PLAYER:

DATE	TIME	FIELD

TEAM _____

PLAYER:	PLAYER:

PLAYER:	PLAYER:

PLAYER:	PLAYER:

TEAM	-	
CATEGORY	COMPETITION	

TEAM _____

N	PLAYER	DEM.	FIRST GLANCE
1.			
2.			
3.			
4.			
5.			
6.			
7.			
8.			
9.			
10.			
11.			
12.			
13.			
14.			
15.			
16.			
17.			
18.			

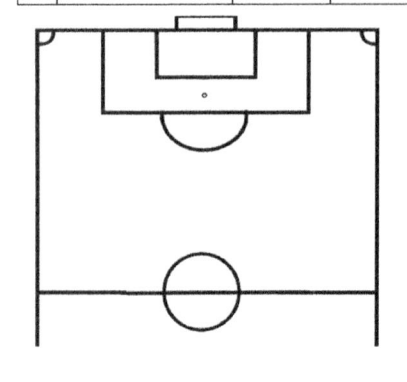

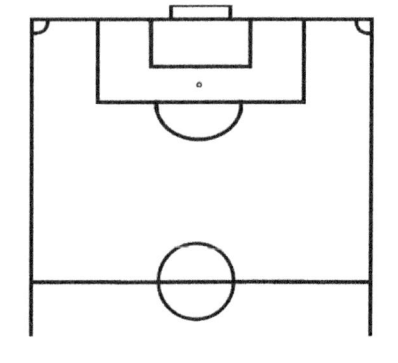

DATE	TIME	FIELD
Observation (direct / video):		

Referencias de jugadores/as del EQUIPO _____

N	PLAYER	DEM.	FIRST GLANCE
1.			
2.			
3.			
4.			
5.			
6.			
7.			
8.			
9.			
10.			
11.			
12.			
13.			
14.			
15.			
16.			
17.			
18.			

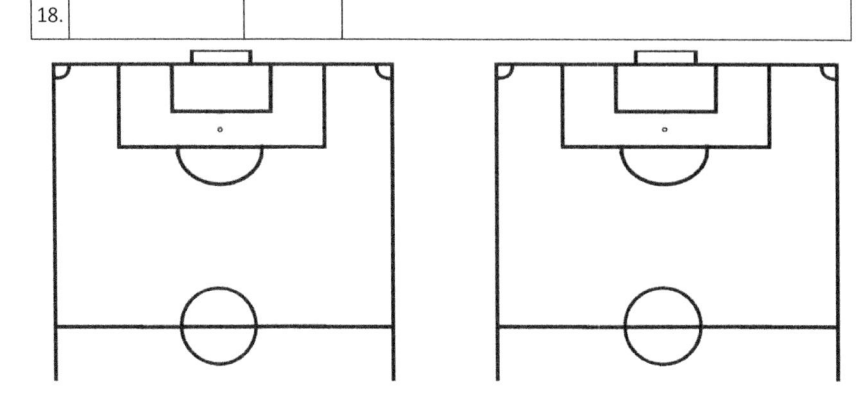

MATCH	-
CATEGORY	COMPETITION

TEAM _____

PLAYER:	PLAYER:

PLAYER:	PLAYER:

PLAYER:	PLAYER:

DATE	TIME	FIELD

TEAM _____

PLAYER:

PLAYER:

PLAYER:

PLAYER:

PLAYER:

PLAYER:

TEAM	-	
CATEGORY	COMPETITION	

TEAM _____

N	PLAYER	DEM.	FIRST GLANCE
1.			
2.			
3.			
4.			
5.			
6.			
7.			
8.			
9.			
10.			
11.			
12.			
13.			
14.			
15.			
16.			
17.			
18.			

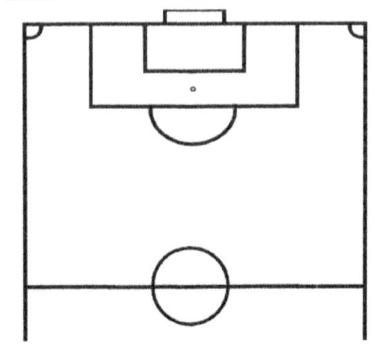

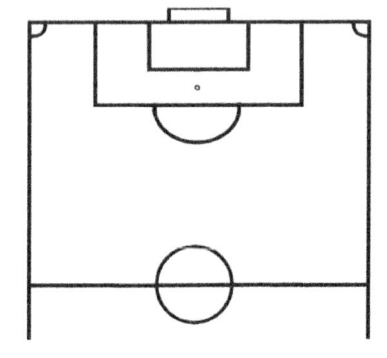

DATE	TIME	FIELD
Observation (direct / video):		

Referencias de jugadores/as del EQUIPO _____

N	PLAYER	DEM.	FIRST GLANCE
1.			
2.			
3.			
4.			
5.			
6.			
7.			
8.			
9.			
10.			
11.			
12.			
13.			
14.			
15.			
16.			
17.			
18.			

MATCH	-
CATEGORY	COMPETITION

TEAM _____

PLAYER:	PLAYER:
PLAYER:	**PLAYER:**
PLAYER:	**PLAYER:**

DATE	TIME	FIELD

TEAM _____

PLAYER:	PLAYER:

PLAYER:	PLAYER:

PLAYER:	PLAYER:

TEAM	-
CATEGORY	COMPETITION

TEAM _____

N	PLAYER	DEM.	FIRST GLANCE
1.			
2.			
3.			
4.			
5.			
6.			
7.			
8.			
9.			
10.			
11.			
12.			
13.			
14.			
15.			
16.			
17.			
18.			

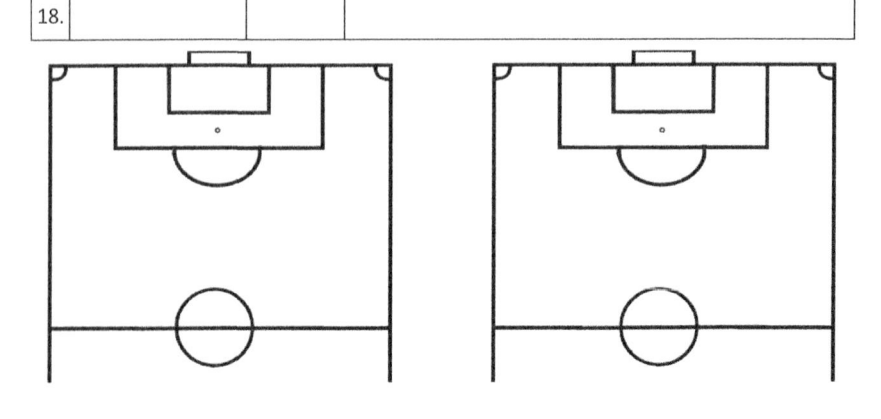

DATE	TIME	FIELD
Observation (direct / video):		

Referencias de jugadores/as del EQUIPO _____

N	PLAYER	DEM.	FIRST GLANCE
1.			
2.			
3.			
4.			
5.			
6.			
7.			
8.			
9.			
10.			
11.			
12.			
13.			
14.			
15.			
16.			
17.			
18.			

MATCH	-
CATEGORY	COMPETITION

TEAM _____

PLAYER:	PLAYER:

PLAYER:	PLAYER:

PLAYER:	PLAYER:

DATE	TIME	FIELD

TEAM _____

PLAYER:	PLAYER:

PLAYER:	PLAYER:

PLAYER:	PLAYER:

TEAM	-	
CATEGORY		COMPETITION

TEAM _____

N	PLAYER	DEM.	FIRST GLANCE
1.			
2.			
3.			
4.			
5.			
6.			
7.			
8.			
9.			
10.			
11.			
12.			
13.			
14.			
15.			
16.			
17.			
18.			

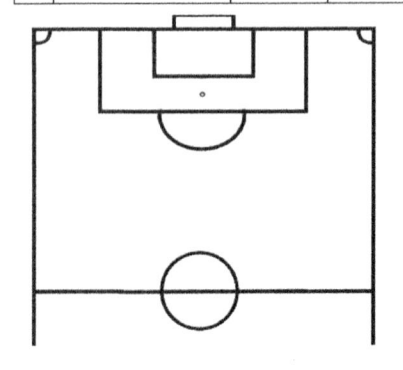

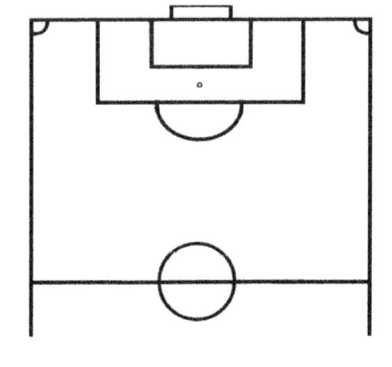

DATE	TIME	FIELD
Observation (direct / video):		

Referencias de jugadores/as del EQUIPO _____

N	PLAYER	DEM.	FIRST GLANCE
1.			
2.			
3.			
4.			
5.			
6.			
7.			
8.			
9.			
10.			
11.			
12.			
13.			
14.			
15.			
16.			
17.			
18.			

MATCH	-
CATEGORY	COMPETITION

TEAM _____

PLAYER:	PLAYER:

PLAYER:	PLAYER:

PLAYER:	PLAYER:

DATE	TIME	FIELD

TEAM _____

PLAYER:	PLAYER:

PLAYER:	PLAYER:

PLAYER:	PLAYER:

TEAM	-	
CATEGORY	COMPETITION	

TEAM _____

N	PLAYER	DEM.	FIRST GLANCE
1.			
2.			
3.			
4.			
5.			
6.			
7.			
8.			
9.			
10.			
11.			
12.			
13.			
14.			
15.			
16.			
17.			
18.			

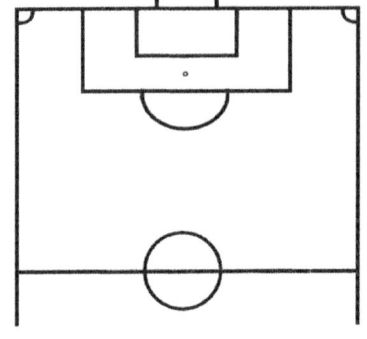

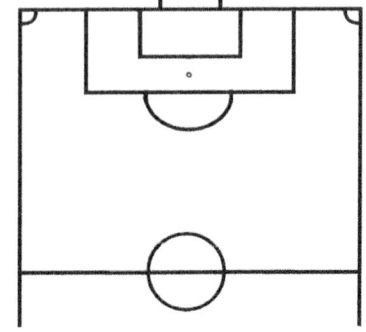

DATE	TIME	FIELD
Observation (direct / video):		

Referencias de jugadores/as del EQUIPO _____

N	PLAYER	DEM.	FIRST GLANCE
1.			
2.			
3.			
4.			
5.			
6.			
7.			
8.			
9.			
10.			
11.			
12.			
13.			
14.			
15.			
16.			
17.			
18.			

MATCH	-
CATEGORY	COMPETITION

TEAM _____

PLAYER:	PLAYER:

PLAYER:	PLAYER:

PLAYER:	PLAYER:

DATE	TIME	FIELD

TEAM _____

PLAYER:

PLAYER:

PLAYER:

PLAYER:

PLAYER:

PLAYER:

TEAM	-
CATEGORY	COMPETITION

TEAM _____

N	PLAYER	DEM.	FIRST GLANCE
1.			
2.			
3.			
4.			
5.			
6.			
7.			
8.			
9.			
10.			
11.			
12.			
13.			
14.			
15.			
16.			
17.			
18.			

DATE	TIME	FIELD
Observation (direct / video):		

Referencias de jugadores/as del EQUIPO _____

N	PLAYER	DEM.	FIRST GLANCE
1.			
2.			
3.			
4.			
5.			
6.			
7.			
8.			
9.			
10.			
11.			
12.			
13.			
14.			
15.			
16.			
17.			
18.			

MATCH	-
CATEGORY	COMPETITION

TEAM _____

PLAYER:	PLAYER:

PLAYER:	PLAYER:

PLAYER:	PLAYER:

DATE	TIME	FIELD

TEAM _____

PLAYER:	PLAYER:

PLAYER:	PLAYER:

PLAYER:	PLAYER:

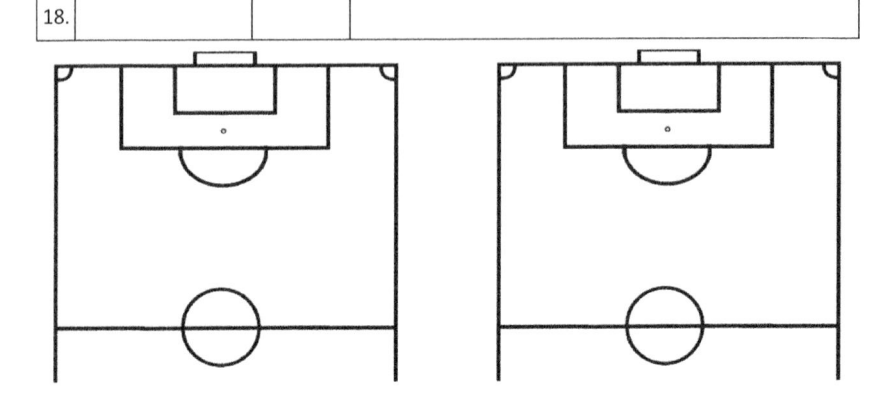

TEAM	-	
CATEGORY	COMPETITION	

TEAM _____

N	PLAYER	DEM.	FIRST GLANCE
1.			
2.			
3.			
4.			
5.			
6.			
7.			
8.			
9.			
10.			
11.			
12.			
13.			
14.			
15.			
16.			
17.			
18.			

DATE	TIME	FIELD
Observation (direct / video):		

Referencias de jugadores/as del EQUIPO _____

N	PLAYER	DEM.	FIRST GLANCE
1.			
2.			
3.			
4.			
5.			
6.			
7.			
8.			
9.			
10.			
11.			
12.			
13.			
14.			
15.			
16.			
17.			
18.			

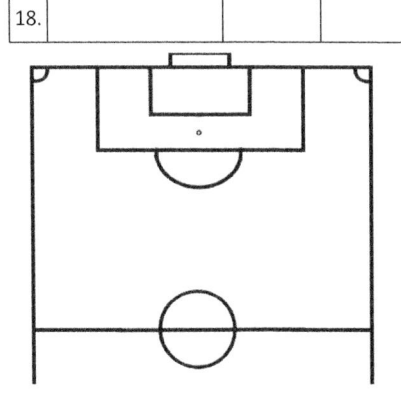

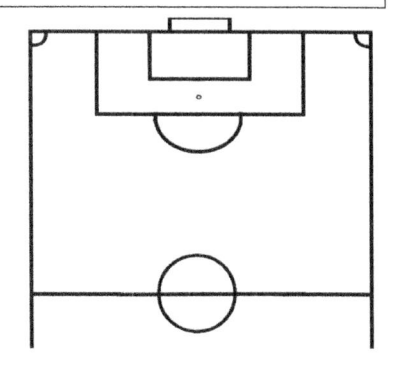

MATCH	-
CATEGORY	COMPETITION

TEAM _____

PLAYER:	PLAYER:

PLAYER:	PLAYER:

PLAYER:	PLAYER:

DATE	TIME	FIELD

TEAM _____

PLAYER:

PLAYER:

PLAYER:

PLAYER:

PLAYER:

PLAYER:

Printed in Great Britain
by Amazon